SLED DOGS ON THE JOB

BY ALLAN MOREY

The Child's World®
childsworld.com

Published by The Child's World®
1980 Lookout Drive • Mankato, MN 56003-1705
800-599-READ • www.childsworld.com

Photographs ©: Colombo Nicola/Shutterstock Images, cover, 1; iStockphoto, 5, 6; Jeff Schultz/Newscom, 9; Nadezda Murmakova/Shutterstock Images, 10; JasperImage/Shutterstock Images, 12; Andrey Kuzmin/Shutterstock Images, 13; Martina I. Meyer/Shutterstock Images, 14; Shutterstock Images, 17, 20; Design Pics Inc/Alamy, 18

ISBN 9781503816176

LCCN 2016945604

Printed in the United States of America
PA02318

TABLE OF CONTENTS

FAST FACTS

The Job

- Sled dogs work together to pull a sled.
- People use dogsleds to travel and to carry supplies over snow and ice. Sled dogs can be more reliable in bad weather than airplanes or snowmobiles.
- Each dog in a sled dog team has a different job. Lead dogs have the most important task. They follow a person's commands and set the pace.

Training Time

- Sled dogs often start basic training at eight weeks old.
- Most sled dogs are ready to join a team after approximately two years of training. Lead dogs may train for even longer.

Common Breeds

- Alaskan malamute
- Siberian husky
- Canadian Eskimo dog

Famous Sled Dogs

- Togo and Balto led a famous trip to carry medicine to Nome, Alaska, in 1925. They helped inspire the Iditarod sled dog race.

Chapter 1

RACE TO NOME, ALASKA

A bad disease hit Nome, Alaska, in December 1924. It was a **diphtheria** outbreak. The town's doctor did not have medicine to treat everyone. Many people were at risk of getting sick and possibly dying.

Alaska's governor quickly worked on a plan to get more medicine to Nome. Planes could not make the flight in winter. The closest railroad ended in Nenana, Alaska. This was 674 miles (1,085 km) away from Nome. No roads went all the way to Nome. The land was covered in ice and snow. The only way to get medicine to Nome was by dogsled.

◀ Sled dogs are used to transport people and objects across difficult terrain.

William "Wild Bill" Shannon picked up the medicine at the Nenana train station on January 27, 1925. Normally, the trip to Nome took two weeks. But the people of Nome could not wait that long.

Shannon started the journey with his nine sled dogs. Frigid winds gusted. Blackie was Shannon's lead dog. Blackie led the team through the night. Along the way, several tired dogs had to be left behind. Shannon got **frostbite**. After a 52-mile (84-km) run, the team passed on the medicine to the next dogsled team.

Through blizzards and subzero temperatures, the race to Nome continued. The medicine was passed from one dogsled team to the next. The dogs ran past the point of exhaustion. Many were left behind. Several dogs died.

On January 31, it was Togo's turn. Togo had won many sled dog races. His **musher** was Leonhard Seppala. The pair had to lead the team through the most dangerous part of the trip. They picked up the medicine along the western shore of Norton **Sound**.

They set out across frozen water to its northern shore. They had 91 miles (146 km) to go before handing off the medicine to the next team. To make matters worse, a fierce storm was heading their way.

▲ Mushers must be careful not to fall through thin ice when traveling across bodies of water such as the Norton Sound.

Chapter 2

SLED DOG TRAINING

Like all sled dogs, Togo needed a lot of training before he became a lead dog. His training started when he was a puppy.

The best time for sled dog puppies to be born is in the spring. This way, their mother has time to recover before training starts in late summer. The puppies also have to grow enough to begin training by the time the snow falls.

At about eight weeks, a musher starts a puppy's training. First, he teaches it basic **obedience**. He also has the puppy wear a **harness**. The puppy keeps the harness on for a short time each day and gets used to the straps around its chests and shoulders.

◄ **A harness helps put the weight of the object the dog is pulling on the dog's chest and shoulders.**

The puppy also gets used to the harness tightening when the musher pulls on the leash.

After four months, the musher has the puppy pull the track of a snowmobile. The track is light, and it rolls smoothly. It does not bounce and scare the puppy when pulled. The musher uses treats to get the puppy to pull.

▲ In summer and fall, mushers can train their dogs by having them pull carts or bicycles.

▲ **New sled dogs can sometimes get distracted by other dogs.**

The puppy chases after the treats and pulls the sled. Eventually the puppy learns to lead. It pulls while the musher walks behind it.

As the puppy gets comfortable pulling, the musher teaches it commands. The puppy learns that *gee* means to turn right. *Haw* means to turn left. The commands are difficult to learn, so the musher takes things slowly. He wants the puppy to feel confident before the next stage of training. After several months, the puppy is ready to help pull a sled. The musher puts the youngster with experienced dogs.

Chapter 3

HARNESSING A SLED DOG TEAM

As the musher gets the sled ready, the dogs bark and yip. They are excited to get on the trail. The musher harnesses the dogs in pairs. The dogs are positioned based on their traits and experience. First the musher hooks up the lead dogs. They are at the very front. These are the musher's smartest and most experienced dogs. They have the job of listening to commands.

"Line out!" the musher shouts. The lead dogs pull the line tight. This helps with harnessing the rest of the team. Next the musher hooks up the swing dogs. This pair is placed right behind the lead dogs. They will help steer the sled.

◂ Sled dogs are paired based on their skills and levels of experience.

Then come the team dogs. Some mushers use several pairs of team dogs for long trips. Team dogs are the main pulling dogs. They also help maintain the sled's speed. Lastly, the musher hooks up the largest and strongest dogs. They are called wheel dogs. During climbs, they pull most of the sled's weight.

When all is ready, the musher hops on the sled. The lead dogs leap into action. The wheel dogs tug. The sled lurches forward. Soon the sled is whisking through the snow. "Haw!" the musher commands. The lead dogs follow the trail to the left. The swing dogs pull the other dogs in that direction. Then the team races up a hill. The wheel dogs muscle the sled forward. The team dogs help keep the sled moving.

At the end of the trail, the musher yells, "Whoa!" The dogs slow to a stop. They pant puffs of steam after their run. The musher gives each dog a treat for doing a good job. The dogs are starting to work as a team!

Each sled dog's harness is connected to a cord in the center, called a gang line. ▶

Chapter 4

THE FINAL LEG

Leonhard Seppala's team could not have had a better lead dog. Togo led the dogs fearlessly into the storm. Winds gusted and temperatures dropped as the dogs ran through the night. Seppala could not see where he was going because of the swirling snow. But Togo led his team onward. The dogs raced for 91 miles (147 km) across the Norton Sound. They arrived in the town of Golovin the morning of February 1.

After one other musher, the medicine was handed off to Gunnar Kaason. His lead dog was Balto. The storm still raged on. Through the gusting wind and snow, Kaason could barely see the dogs harnessed to his sled.

◀ **Leonhard Seppala with his team of sled dogs**

▲ **Every year, mushers from around the world commemorate the dogsled relay of 1925 with a race in Alaska.**

He had to trust Balto to lead the way. They raced 54 miles (87 km) on the final leg of the **relay**.

After five and a half days, the medicine arrived in Nome. Normally this trip took 14 days.

Because he led the last leg of the relay, Balto became a hero. But he was just one of approximately 150 dogs that helped save the day.

THINK ABOUT IT

- Other forms of transportation are faster than sled dog teams. But sled dogs are still used today. Can you think of cases where it would be better to travel by dogsled than by other means of transportation?
- A movie has been made about Balto. There is also a statue honoring him in New York City's Central Park. Does he deserve more recognition than the other dogs?
- The Iditarod sled dog race honors the brave dogs that saved people in Nome. What would it be like to be a musher on the Iditarod?

GLOSSARY

diphtheria (dif-THIR-ee-ah): Diphtheria is a contagious disease that makes it difficult to breathe. A diphtheria outbreak threatened the people of Nome, Alaska.

frostbite (FRAWST-bite): Frostbite is a condition in which parts of the body freeze or almost freeze. During the trip from Nenana to Nome, several mushers suffered frostbite.

harness (HAHR-nuhss): A harness is a set of straps that a dog is fastened to when pulling a sled. A sled dog's harness is attached to the sled with a leash.

musher (MUSH-ur): A musher is a dogsled driver. A musher tells a sled dog team what to do.

obedience (oh-BEE-dee-ens): Obedience is the act of following directions. A musher teaches sled dogs obedience.

relay (REE-lay): A relay is a race in which members of a team each run a leg of the race. Mushers used a relay to get medicine from Nenana to Nome.

sound (SOUND): A sound is a narrow arm of water between two larger bodies of water or between an island and the mainland. Mushers crossed the Norton Sound.

TO LEARN MORE

Books

Blake, Kevin. *Balto's Story*. New York: Bearport, 2015.

Funk, Joe. *Mush! Sled Dogs of the Iditarod*. New York: Scholastic, 2013.

Rajczak, Kristen. *Racing the Iditarod*. New York: Gareth Stevens, 2014.

Web Sites

Visit our Web site for links about sled dogs:
childsworld.com/links

Note to Parents, Teachers, and Librarians: We routinely verify our Web links to make sure they are safe and active sites. So encourage your readers to check them out!

SELECTED BIBLIOGRAPHY

Klein, Christopher. "The Sled Dog Relay That Inspired the Iditarod." *History.com*. A&E Networks, 10 Mar. 2014. Web. 22 Jun. 2016.

Lee, Jane J. "What Makes a Great Sled Dog? Breed, Ambition, Tough Feet." *National Geographic*. National Geographic Society, 31 Jan. 2015. Web. 22 Jun. 2016.

Neary, Kathleen Seiler. "How Sled Dogs Work." *HowStuffWorks.com*. InfoSpace, 2016. Web. 22 Jun. 2016.

"Sled Dogs: An Alaskan Epic." *Nature*. PBS, 21 Nov. 1999. Web. 22 Jun. 2016.

INDEX

ABOUT THE AUTHOR

Allan Morey grew up on a farm in central Wisconsin, which is where his love of animals began. He has had pet pigs, chickens, rabbits, ferrets, cats, and many other animals. He now lives in Saint Paul, Minnesota, with his wife, two kids, and of course, a couple of dogs.